TURKEY

Big Buddy Books
An Imprint of Abdo Publishing
www.abdopublishing.com

Julie Murray

www.abdopublishing.com

Published by Abdo Publishing, a division of ABDO, PO Box 398166, Minneapolis, Minnesota 55439.
Copyright © 2015 by Abdo Consulting Group, Inc. International copyrights reserved in all countries. No part of this book may be reproduced in any form without written permission from the publisher. Big Buddy Books™ is a trademark and logo of Abdo Publishing.

Printed in the United States of America, North Mankato, Minnesota.
032014
092014

THIS BOOK CONTAINS
RECYCLED MATERIALS

Cover Photo: Shutterstock.
Interior Photos: AFP/Getty Images (p. 34), ASSOCIATED PRESS (pp. 16, 17, 19, 29, 31, 33), iStockphoto (pp. 13, 15, 25, 29), Shutterstock (pp. 5, 9, 11, 13, 19, 21, 23, 27, 34, 35, 37, 38).

Coordinating Series Editor: Rochelle Baltzer
Editor: Sarah Tieck
Contributing Editors: Bridget O'Brien, Marcia Zappa
Graphic Design: Adam Craven

Country population and area figures taken from the CIA World Factbook.

Library of Congress Cataloging-in-Publication Data

Murray, Julie, 1969-
  Turkey / Julie Murray.
      pages cm. -- (Explore the countries)
  ISBN 978-1-62403-348-3
  1. Turkey--Juvenile literature. I. Title.
  DR417.4.M87 2014
   956.1--dc23
                              2013051239

TURKEY

CONTENTS

Around the World

Our world has many countries. Each country has beautiful land. It has its own rich history. And, the people have their own languages and ways of life.

Turkey is a country with parts in both Europe and Asia. What do you know about Turkey? Let's learn more about this place and its story!

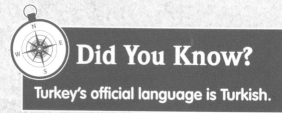
Did You Know?
Turkey's official language is Turkish.

Bodies of water split the part of Turkey in Europe from the part in Asia.

PASSPORT TO TURKEY

Turkey is in a part of the world known as the Middle East. Eight countries and three seas border it. Turkey's total area is 302,535 square miles (783,562 sq km). About 81.6 million people live there.

WHERE IN THE WORLD?

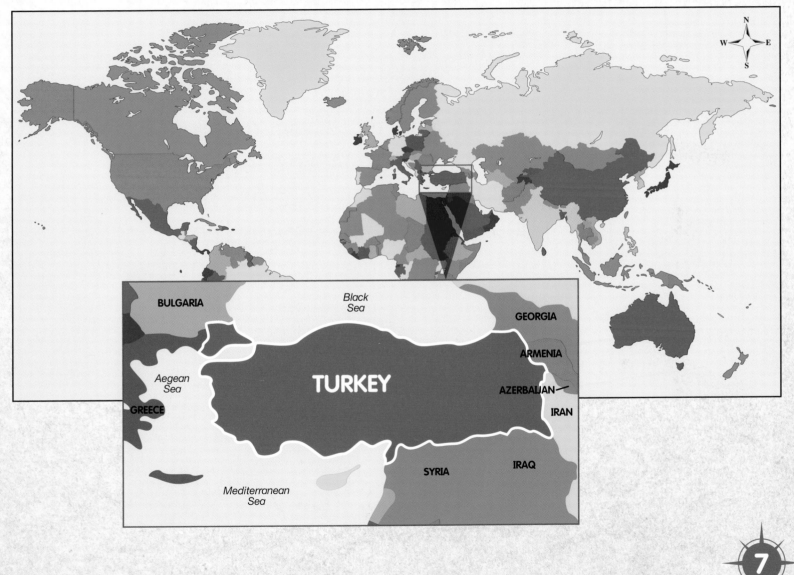

BULGARIA

Black
Sea

GEORGIA

Aegean
Sea

TURKEY

ARMENIA

AZERBAIJAN

GREECE

IRAN

SYRIA

IRAQ

Mediterranean
Sea

IMPORTANT CITIES

Istanbul is Turkey's largest city. There are more than 13.7 million people in the city and its nearby areas.

Istanbul's history dates to before 600 BC. This old city has more than 1,000 beautiful palaces and churches. Today, people visit the city's museums and bazaars.

SAY IT

Istanbul
ihs-tuhn-BOOL

bazaar
buh-ZAHR

Istanbul's Grand Bazaar has goods including jewelry, carpets, and spices.

TURKEY

Istanbul
★Ankara
Izmir

The Golden Horn is a body of water that runs through the city.

Ankara is Turkey's **capital** and second-largest city. More than 4.6 million people live in the city and its nearby areas. Many of the city's people work for the government.

Izmir is Turkey's third-largest city. The city and its nearby areas have about 3.4 million people. The city has an important port. Fruit, cotton, and olive oil are among the goods shipped from there.

Did You Know?

Ankara became Turkey's capital in 1923.

SAY IT

Ankara
ANG-kuh-ruh

Izmir
ihz-MIHR

Aegean
ih-JEE-uhn

Ankara has a fortress on top of a hill. It was once used to help guard the city.

People visit Izmir to spend time at the Aegean Sea.

Turkey in History

Around 6700 BC people built a settlement in what is now Turkey. It was called Çatalhüyük. The Hittites came to the area around 2000 BC. Soon, they ruled the Middle East.

By the first century BC, Turkey was part of the Roman **Empire**. Constantine the Great made the town of Byzantium the empire's **capital**. He changed its name to Constantinople. In 395, the empire split. Turkey stayed part of the Byzantine Empire.

Çatalhüyük
cha-TAHL-hoo-YOOK

Hittites
HIH-tites

Byzantium
buh-ZAN-tee-uhm

Scientists have uncovered old buildings from Çatalhüyük.

Constantine the Great brought the Serpentine Column to what is now Istanbul.

The Seljuk Turks were the first Turkish people to rule what is now Turkey. These **Muslims** took power in areas around Constantinople.

By the late 1300s, this area was taken over by a group of Turks known as Ottomans. In 1453, Ottomans **conquered** Constantinople. They renamed the city Istanbul and made it their **capital**. Turkey became independent in 1923.

In the 1200s, travelers rested at roadside inns in central Turkey. The remains of these can be seen today.

TIMELINE

1776

Some stories say candy maker Bekir Effendi opened his shop in Istanbul. He made a flavored candy called Turkish delight.

334 BC

Alexander the Great took over most of modern Turkey. He was an ancient king.

1361

Edirne hosted its first Turkish wrestling match. This is said to be the world's oldest continual sporting event.

1908

Aleko Mulas **competed** in gymnastics during Turkey's first time at the Olympics.

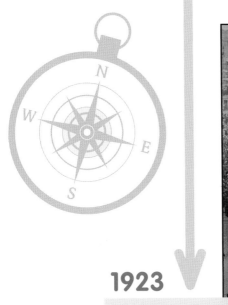

1923

Turkey became a **republic** on October 29.

2013

People protested against Turkey's government across the country.

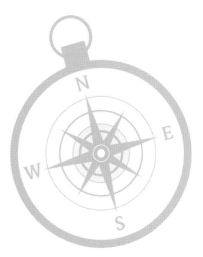

An Important Symbol

Turkey's flag was adopted in 1936. The background is red. In the center is a white moon and star.

Turkey's government is a **republic**. The Grand National Assembly makes laws. The prime minister is the head of government. The president is the head of state.

The moon and star stand for the Islam religion.

Abdullah Gul became Turkey's president in 2007.

ACROSS THE LAND

Turkey has grasslands, mountains, and beaches. Its highest mountain is Mount Ararat.

Much of Turkey borders water. The Black Sea is a large body of salt water to the north. It is connected to the Mediterranean Sea.

Did You Know?

In January, Istanbul's average high temperature is about 46°F (8°C). In July, it is about 84°F (29°C).

Mount Ararat is in eastern Turkey. It rises 16,946 feet (5,165 m).

Turkey's animals include goats, wildcats, and snakes. Dolphins, turtles, and many kinds of fish live in the water. Birds such as ducks, geese, and herons travel through the area.

Turkey's land is home to a wide variety of plants. Grasses grow in the dry areas. Oak, juniper, and pine trees grow near the coasts.

Anatolian shepherd dogs are a famous breed of dog from Turkey. They help keep sheep and goat herds safe.

Earning a Living

Turkey's **economy** is growing. The government runs some businesses. Many people have jobs helping visitors to the country. Turkey's factories make food, drinks, and cloth.

Turkey has some **natural resources**. Chromite and boron come from its mines. Farmers grow grains, cotton, fruits, nuts, and vegetables. They raise cattle, chickens, and sheep.

LIFE IN TURKEY

Most people in Turkey live in cities and towns. Others live on farms or in small villages. In cities, most people live in apartments. In villages, people live in cottages or small houses.

Turks commonly eat wheat bread and rice. A meal may include shish kebabs. These have lamb and vegetables on a stick. Borek and baklava are popular baked goods. And, people drink tea and coffee.

Turkish delight is a favorite candy. It comes in many flavors.

Turks enjoy playing soccer. Wrestling is another popular sport. People play dice games or card games. Turkish people also enjoy movies and concerts.

Many Turks are **Muslims**. But, people are free to choose any religion. Another common religion in Turkey is the Eastern Orthodox Church.

Turkish people visit with friends at coffee houses.

Muslim women often cover their hair and neck as a sign of modesty.

FAMOUS FACES

Kemal Atatürk was born Mustafa Kemal in 1881. His birthplace was Salonika, Greece.

In 1923, Atatürk founded the **Republic** of Turkey. He was its first president. He served until his death in 1938.

Atatürk helped create Turkey's government and laws. This government started businesses, improved schools, and gave women the right to vote.

Atatürk was a powerful military leader. He helped Turkey fight for its independence.

Did You Know?

Atatürk chose his last name. It means "father of the Turks."

Orhan Pamuk was born on June 7, 1952, in Istanbul. He is one of Turkey's most famous writers.

Pamuk wrote his first novel in 1982. His stories are often about Turkish people. In 2006, he won the Nobel Prize in literature. He was the first Turk to be honored in this way.

Through his writing, Pamuk shared new ideas about how people live in Turkey.

TOUR BOOK

Imagine traveling to Turkey! Here are some places you could go and things you could do.

🧭 Celebrate

April 23 is National Sovereignty and Children's Day. Children attend special events and visit government offices on this day.

🧭 Explore

Visit Pamukkale's hot spring pools. They are believed to have healing powers. People can swim in the pools.

 Play

Splash in the gentle waters of Ölüdeniz. This village is on the Aegean Sea. Many people like to paraglide there.

See

Visit Ephesus, near Izmir in western Turkey. This was once an important Greek city.

Discover

Hagia Sophia is a famous domed building in Istanbul. It was built as a church during the 500s.

A Great Country

The story of Turkey is important to our world. Turkey is a land of historic buildings and popular beaches. It is a country formed from strong leaders.

The people and places that make up Turkey offer something special. They help make the world a more beautiful, interesting place.

The Blue Mosque was built in the 1600s. It is called that for its blue tiles inside.

Turkey Up Close

Official Name: Türkiye Cumhuriyeti
(Republic of Turkey)

Flag:

Population (rank): 81,619,392
(July 2014 est.)
(17th most-populated country)

Total Area (rank): 302,535 square miles
(37th largest country)

Capital: Ankara

Official Language: Turkish

Currency: Turkish lira

Form of Government: Republic

National Anthem: "Istiklal Marsi"
(Independence March)

IMPORTANT WORDS

capital a city where government leaders meet.

compete to take part in a contest between two or more persons or groups.

conquer (KAHN-kuhr) to take control using military force.

economy the way that a country produces, sells, and buys goods and services.

empire a large group of states or countries under one ruler called an emperor or empress.

Muslim a person who practices Islam, which is a religion based on a belief in Allah as God and Muhammad as his prophet.

natural resources useful and valued supplies from nature.

republic a government in which the people choose the leader.

WEBSITES

To learn more about Explore the Countries, visit **booklinks.abdopublishing.com**. These links are routinely monitored and updated to provide the most current information available.

INDEX